Float Fishing Tackle and Techniques for Stillwaters and Rivers

PAUL DUFFIELD

CONTENTS

INTRODUCTION

The term 'float fishing' can be deceptive as it implies that it is a single, perhaps even a simple technique used by anglers to catch coarse fish, but nothing could be further from the truth.

An accomplished angler who can catch fish using a float in a wide variety of waters and conditions uses a range of skills and experience gained over many fishing sessions.

Fly fishing is often held up as the most skilful form of angling, but as someone who enjoys both a coarse and game fishing, I strongly believe that an angler who can control a float in moving water while at the same time feeding bait to keep fish in the swim is every bit as skilful as any angler fishing a fly to catch salmon or trout.

In contrast, many forms of float fishing, especially on stillwaters, use quite simple techniques that can be mastered very quickly by even the most inexperienced angler.

Whether your preference is for large or small stillwater fisheries, deep slow moving rivers or small overgrown rivers and streams, this book will provide information and guidance on tackle, floats, shotting patterns and techniques that will help you to be a successful float angler.

FLOAT FISHING TACKLE

You can float fish with almost any rod and reel, but a rod designed for the job will be easier and more comfortable to use.

CHOOSING A ROD FOR FLOAT FISHING

There are three important considerations to take into account when choosing a rod for float fishing, it needs to be:

- Long enough to enable you to control your float tackle in a wide range of fishing conditions.

- Flexible enough to cast light floats quite long distances and cushion the strike when using light hooklengths.

- Powerful enough to land the largest fish you are likely to catch.

A general purpose float fishing rod of about 12 feet (3.6 metres) in length will cover a wide range of waters. There is a huge range of good quality float rods and any rod of this length described as either a 'float rod' or 'match rod' made using carbon fibre will be suitable for catching fish from a few ounces up to 5 pounds or so.

If the waters you intend to fish hold larger specimens such as barbel or carp up to low double figures, a more powerful rod usually described as an 'Avon' rod with a test curve of around 1.5 pounds will be a better choice.

If you plan to mainly fish commercial carp fisheries, one of the wide range of pellet feeder rods that have been introduced in recent years will be suitable.

For small rivers where a rod of 12 feet (3.6 metres) would be difficult to use because of overgrown banks and overhanging trees, a shorter rod will be easier to handle, but will need to incorporate both a sensitive tip and the power to subdue larger fish such as chub that are often found in such rivers.

At one time it was difficult to find rods around 10 feet (3 metres) that had these qualities, but the shorter pellet waggler rods introduced in recent years for use on carp fisheries are ideal, combining the power to subdue quite large fish with sensitive tip actions.

CHOOSING A REEL FOR FLOAT FISHING

Reel choice is less important and a general purpose fixed spool reel with a spare spool so you can carry different strengths of line will cover float fishing on both stillwaters and rivers.

Some float anglers prefer a centrepin reel for river work. While these can allow for better presentation in some conditions, they are less versatile than a fixed spool reel and harder to use so I suggest waiting until you can fish comfortably with a fixed spool reel before trying a centrepin.

PARTS OF A FIXED SPOOL REEL

1: Pick up or bail
2: Reel seat
3: Reel foot
4: Handle
5: Support arm
6: Anti-reverse lever
7: Skirted spool
8: Fishing line
9: Drag/clutch adjustment knob

LINE FOR YOUR REEL

If you have two spools a line of 3lbs (1.4 kg) will cover a wide range of float fishing situations, and one of 6lbs (2.7 kg) will be suitable for waters where there is the possibility of a larger fish coming along.

There are many manufacturers of line and the price can vary significantly, but a mid-price line is fine to begin with and will usually be more forgiving in use than the more expensive specialist lines.

You will need 100 metres of line in each of the strengths that you choose and any line described as 'monofilament' or 'nylon' in strengths approximating those above will be suitable.

LOADING LINE ON TO THE REEL

Line should be loaded on to the reel so that it almost reaches the edge of the spool.

A reel that is not loaded with enough line will be difficult to cast with while an overfilled spool will result in tangles.

UNDERFILLED   OVERFILLED   CORRECT

Some reels have narrow spools that only need 100 metres of line to fill them, but others have deep spools and these need to be loaded with backing before attaching the fishing line. You can buy specialist backing, but any old line will do to fill out a spool if you have some.

An alternative to using backing or old line is to wrap self-adhesive tape around the spool, but if you do this, make sure that you apply the tape uniformly so the line will wind evenly on to the spool.

LINE FOR HOOK LENGTHS

If you plan to tie your own hooks you will need line for hook lengths that is slightly weaker than the main line attached to the reel. This is so that in the event of the line breaking, either due to an unexpectedly large fish or by being caught on an obstruction either in or out of the water, only the short length of line attached to the hook will be lost, resulting in less tackle lost or left attached to a fish.

You will see lines for sale described as for 'hook lengths' but in practice any line that is suitable as reel line will be suitable. In general a hook length of .5 lb (.23 kg) to 1lb (.45 kg) lighter than the reel line will be fine for most situations, but you may need to use a lighter line with small hooks or on hard fished waters.

If you only intend to use hooks already tied to nylon hook lengths, choose those which are tied to line that is lighter than the main line you intend using.

FISHING FLOATS

If you look at the floats on offer in a fishing tackle shop you will see that there is a huge variety of floats designed to cover every imaginable fishing situation.

You do need a variety of floats if you plan to fish a range of different waters, but a few basic patterns and sizes will be sufficient to begin with.

I will cover float choice for different waters and conditions in more detail later, but in this section I will describe the floats you will need to buy depending on the types of waters you intend to fish.

I will divide these into two broad categories, floats for stillwaters such as lakes, ponds and canals and floats for rivers. If you intend to fish both still and running water you will need a selection from both categories, otherwise you will just need a range of floats from the category for the type of water you intend to fish.

FLOATS FOR STILLWATERS

Most stillwater floats are collectively known as wagglers. These are straight floats with variations such a thinner section of material inserted at the tip (insert wagglers) or a body of cork, balsa or polystyrene near the base (bodied wagglers).

Waggler floats are usually attached to the line at the bottom only, locked in place by shot. Examples of shotting patterns for these floats will be covered in detail later.

A range of insert wagglers in lengths from 5 to 9 inches (12 to 23cm) carrying shot between 2AAA and 6AAA will cover most stillwater angling situations. Complete your stillwater float collection with a few more floats covering the variations described below and you will be well equipped for most stillwaters.

INSERT WAGGLER

A sensitive float usually made from cane, peacock quill or plastic with a straight or slightly tapered body and incorporating a tip of thinner material inserted into the main float body.

BODIED INSERT WAGGLER

A variation on the insert waggler with a body at the base to provide additional stability and shot carrying capacity.

BODIED WAGGLER

A straight float with a body at the base to provide additional stability and shot carrying capacity.

WINDBEATER

A variation on the bodied waggler with a large sight tip to aid visibility when fishing at extreme range. The large sight tip also allows this float to be fished over-depth as it is not easily pulled under by surface tow. This float is sometimes called a driftbeater.

PELLET WAGGLER

The pellet waggler is a thicker and shorter version of the straight waggler developed for fishing in commercial carp fisheries.

LOADED PELLET WAGGLER

A self-cocking version of the pellet waggler developed for fishing in commercial carp fisheries.

BAGGING WAGGLER

The bagging waggler is a version of the pellet waggler than incorporates a cage around which groundbait can be moulded to feed the swim each time the float is cast.

SPLASHER WAGGLER

The splasher waggler is a specialised version of the pellet waggler developed for use on commercial carp fisheries.

MUSHROOM WAGGLER

The mushroom waggler is a specialised version of the pellet waggler developed for use on commercial carp fisheries.

CARP CONTROLLER

The carp controller is used for fishing a bait on the surface, primarily when fishing for carp.

FLOATS FOR RIVERS

There is some overlap between floats for stillwater and river fishing. Although floats designed specifically for river fishing will probably be those you use the most, there will be times when a straight or insert waggler will be more suitable.

The majority of floats designed for river fishing are attached to the line using silicon tubing at both the top and bottom of the float. Anglers often refer to this as 'top and bottom' or 'double rubber', the latter phrase being from a time when rubber tubing was used in place of silicon.

Although they are all attached to the line and fished in a similar way, there are many different styles of river float, designed to cope with a wide range of fishing conditions.

I will explain the reasons for choosing a specific type of float in detail later, but for now I will describe the main types of river float and suggest which you should buy to ensure you are equipped for the different situations you will encounter.

STICK FLOAT

Stick floats are the most widely used floats for fishing rivers. These are floats constructed in two parts, the top part being of balsa or polystyrene and the bottom of either cane, plastic or wire.

Generally speaking, the further you need to cast, the larger the float you will use, but a small range of stick floats in four or five sizes will be enough to get you started. Avoid the smallest and largest of this type of float, and obtain a few ranging in size from 4 to 6 inches (10 to 15cm) in length.

BALSA FLOAT

These floats are similar in appearance to stick floats, but are more buoyant as they do not incorporate the heavier material in the base that stick floats do. As they take more shot they are suitable for faster water where it is necessary to use a lot of weight to get the bait down to the fish near the bottom.

A range of balsa floats in lengths from 4 to 6 inches (10 to 15cm) will cover most of your angling needs.

AVON FLOAT

These are floats that incorporate a large body of balsa, polystyrene or cork to increase the amount of shot that can be placed on the line. These are mostly used in deeper swims where their extra shot capacity is needed to get the bait down to the fish as quickly as possible.

You will not use these as often as stick floats and balsas, but it is useful to have two or three just in case. A range with shot capacities ranging from 4BB to 6BB will cover most eventualities.

CHUBBER FLOAT

The chubber float is basically a version of the balsa float that is scaled up in width but not length. They carry a much larger amount of shot than a balsa float and are designed primarily to be used with large baits such as lobworms or bread in small and relatively shallow fast flowing rivers.

Unless you intend to specialise in this type of fishing you will rarely, if at all, need to use a chubber, but you may want to carry one or two so you are prepared should the need arise.

STRAIGHT WAGGLER

A simple straight float usually made from reed, peacock quill or plastic. Unlike most river floats, the waggler is attached to line only at the bottom. It is typically used if there is a strong downstream wind and also when fishing very slow rivers or if distance casting is required.

In ideal conditions on slower rivers, the insert version of the waggler described in the section on floats for stillwaters may be used to provide greater sensitivity.

SPECI-WAGGLER

A shorter and thicker version of the straight waggler made from balsa. This float has been developed for fishing shallow swims where the extra thickness and buoyancy allows a shorter float to be used than would be the case with a standard straight waggler.

QUILL FLOATS

Before the development of stick and balsa floats, anglers fished with floats made from bird and porcupine quills. Avon floats incorporating a quill stem are still popular with many anglers and other quill floats can, if you prefer to fish traditionally, be used instead of stick and balsa floats.

As a general guide, floats made from porcupine quill and thin bird quills can be used in place of stick floats, while floats made from thicker quills such as goose and swan can be used in place of balsa and chubber floats.

PACEMAKER AND BIG STICK

You may see variations of the stick and balsa floats described as pacemakers and big sticks. Pacemakers are essentially a thinner version of the balsa while big sticks are thicker bodied versions of the stick float.

Both are useful and effective floats, but if you have a good range of stick and balsa floats you will usually have a float suitable to use in any of the conditions pacemakers and big sticks are designed for.

SHOT

You will need a range of shot in various sizes to give maximum versatility in shotting floats.

There is a wide range of non-toxic shot available, but make sure that you get a good quality brand of soft shot which can usually be identified by a light grey colour. This is less likely to damage line and is easier to remove for re-use.

The sizes most commonly used are SSG, AAA, BBB, Number 1, Number 4, Number 6 and Number 8. You should have no trouble obtaining a single dispenser containing most or all of these sizes.

It is still legal to use lead in size 8 and smaller, but for the larger sizes you must use a non-toxic alternative to lead.

HOOKS

Hook sizes and patterns need to be chosen to match the species of fish and size of bait you intend to use. As a general guide, a selection in sizes 20, 18, 16, 14, 12, 10 and 8 will cover most float fishing situations.

While barbed hooks are still available, some fisheries now insist that only barbless hooks are used, so you should check the rules before you start fishing.

FLOAT CAPS

As explained in the section on river floats, you will need some plastic or silicon tubing in

various thicknesses to attach floats to the line. These are sometimes described as 'float caps' or 'float rubbers'.

You can either buy a packet of pre-cut tubing in mixed sizes, or obtain lengths of plastic or silicon tubing to cut to size when needed.

FLOAT ADAPTERS

Float adapters slip over the stem of waggler floats so that if you want to change to a different float during a session you can do so without having to take everything apart.

These are available either as a single piece of moulded silicon or with a swivel inserted into a length of silicon tube.

These are not essential as most wagglers incorporate a ring for attaching them to the line, but they can save time if a change in conditions means you need to use a heavier float.

PELLET WAGGLER ADAPTERS

Pellet waggler adapters are used to attach loaded pellet wagglers to the line.

PLUMMETS

These are small weights incorporating either a strip of cork or a hinge to hold the hook while lowering the tackle into the swim so you can set the float at the correct depth.

BAIT BANDS

These are silicon bands available in a range of sizes that can be used to attach hard baits such pellets, or large baits such as bread flake to the hook.

SWIVELS

Swivels help to avoid line twist and are used with some specialist carp fishing float rigs.

RUBBER BEADS

Rubber beads are used as a shock absorber with some specialist carp fishing float rigs.

BAITING NEEDLE

If you intend to use hair rigs, a baiting needle with a small hook near the point will be needed to thread baits such as boilies or pellets on to the hair.

ROD RESTS

Rod rests are used to provide a convenient place to put the rod when it is not being held in the hand. When still water float fishing the rod will spend a lot of time in the rests, while for running water fishing they provide a safe and convenient place to put the rod when re-baiting or unhooking a fish.

Rod rests are available either with a male thread to allow them to be screwed into bank sticks, or as a single unit incorporating a 'V' or 'U' shaped rest and a metal pole to be pushed into the river bank.

LANDING NET

A landing net should be regarded as a necessity as any fish over a few ounces in weight will be difficult to land without one.

There are many sizes and types of landing net, but any landing net of about 24 inches (60cm) measured across the widest part will be suitable, with a handle of about 8 feet (2.5 metres).

Check the rules of the waters you intend to fish before buying a net as some will insist that you have a landing net of at least a minimum size before you are allowed to fish for Carp. If you are intending to fish such waters, you will need to obtain two landing nets as the larger nets for carp fishing are not suitable for general coarse fishing.

ADDITIONAL ITEMS

There are many further items that you can buy as part of your fishing kit.

In particular, nail clippers or specialised line cutters will be useful for trimming knots, a disgorger is essential and a pair of forceps will be useful for removing hooks from fish.

A bait waiter to hold a variety of bait near to hand will be useful on some fisheries, a bait apron is useful when fishing rivers if you need to stand or wade and a catapult will be useful for feeding your swim.

If you are likely to catch larger fish such as carp that cannot be easily unhooked in the hand you will need an unhooking mat. Some fisheries may also require that you have other specialist fish care items such as antiseptic.

FLOAT FISHING TECHNIQUES

Float fishing is a generic term for a range of techniques where a baited hook is suspended above the bed of a lake, river or canal using a float made of buoyant material. Shot is used to cause the float to sit in the water with only the tip visible above the surface.

A bite is detected by watching the float for an indication that a fish has taken the bait. The float may be partially or completely submerged, rise out of the water or move across the surface.

Some bites are unmistakable such as when the float sails away beneath the surface, other times, especially when stillwater fishing, you may have to use judgment and experience to decide whether to strike immediately or wait for the bite to develop.

Float fishing is much easier to learn on stillwaters as you do not have to contend with a float moving with the current. Many anglers who have become quite proficient at stillwater fishing never really get to grips with river fishing and resort to legering instead.

While river float fishing does require practice to develop the necessary skills, it only requires the mastery of a few simple techniques to be successful and the results are definitely worth the effort.

FLOAT FISHING ON STILLWATERS

When float fishing on stillwaters such as lakes, ponds and canals the float is attached to the line at the bottom only, locked in place using the bulk of the shot required to set or cock the float. This is often referred to as fishing bottom only.

The remaining shot needed to sink the float so only a little of the tip is showing are then placed on the line between the float and the hook. If you want the bait to sink slowly so that fish feeding up in the water can intercept it, the shot is spaced out, but if you want to get the bait down to the bottom quickly, perhaps because a lot of small fish near the surface are taking the bait before it can reach larger fish below, the shot may need to be bunched closer to the hook.

Unlike in river fishing, which we will cover in a later chapter, when stillwater fishing, the fish alone is responsible for pulling the float down in the water as there is no current, so floats with thin tips, such as the insert waggler described in a previous chapter are often used.

After casting the float to the desired fishing spot, the line needs to be sunk so that the float is not dragged around by surface drift or wind. To do this, immediately after casting drop the tip of the rod in the water and lift it sharply up. This should cause the line between the rod and the float to be pulled beneath the surface. An alternative, if this proves difficult, is to cast beyond the place where you want to fish, and then dip the rod tip in the water, and wind a couple of sharp turns of the reel.

Once the float is in position and the line submerged, the rod should be placed in two rests such that the handle of the rod is conveniently to hand for striking, and the tip is in or near the water to prevent any loose line from being affected by wind.

Watch the float carefully for bites. It may dip quickly under the water, but often you will see the float dip slightly, move to one side, or even come up in the water. All are signals to strike, which should be done by sharply lifting the rod tip up to set the hook.

When fishing a stillwater, the size of float you decide to fish with is determined by the distance you plan to fish at, whether you are casting into a head wind or cross wind and the depth of water.

You should be able to cast comfortably to the place you wish to fish, so if you are finding this difficult or if the wind increases, switch to a larger float or one with a body at the base so you can put more shot on the line. When fishing deep water a larger float may be needed to allow more shot to be placed on the line to get the bait down to the bottom more quickly.

If you need to use a bodied waggler to achieve the distance required, consider whether you can use one with an insert which will be more sensitive, or one without which while being less sensitive will be easier to see and less affected by ripples or waves on the water.

If, after casting, you are having difficulty seeing the float or spotting bites, you can overcome this by using a float with a thicker tip or by increasing the amount of tip showing above the water. Distance fishing can sometimes force you to compromise, sacrificing sensitivity for visibility.

PLUMBING THE DEPTH

You should always find out the depth of the water you are fishing and this can be done quite easily using a plummet.

Set the float at your best guess of the depth of the swim where you intend to fish and attach the plummet to the hook. With an underhand cast, swing the tackle into the water and allow it to settle.

If you have set the float too shallow, it will sink below the surface, if too deep, the float will not settle correctly. Repeat this process until you have found the correct depth and remove the plummet.

Make a note of the depth by winding the float to the top ring of the rod and holding the line parallel to the rod so you can note the position of the hook. If you adjust the depth during a session, by noting the depth against the rod you can easily revert to the plumbed depth.

Some anglers mark the position of the hook with tippex which can be easily scraped off at the end of the session.

ADJUSTING THE DEPTH DURING A SESSION

It is usually best to start by fishing on or near the bottom, but if fish are in the upper levels of water you will often get bites 'on the drop' while the baited hook is falling through the water. If the fish are small, you can move the bulk shot nearer the hook to get a faster fall through the water, or even reduce the size of the locking shot to allow more bulk shot to be placed on the line.

If, on the other hand, it is the fish you wish to catch that are feeding up in the water, moving the shot higher up the line and shortening the line between the float and the hook will ensure that your baited hook stays longer in the feeding zone.

If you are having trouble hitting bites, it pays to adjust the position of the small 'dropper' shot either nearer to the hook or further away until you find the distance that results in the most bites being hit.

While the tackle is in the water, you will keep the bail arm of the reel closed to prevent line being blown off by wind. Whether you also engage the reel's anti-reverse mechanism is a matter of personal choice. If you do, there is no risk of the strike being cushioned by line being pulled off the reel, but you will need to disengage the anti-reverse to play large fish. If you leave the anti-reverse in the off position you will not have to do this, but you will need to trap the spool of the reel with your finger when striking to prevent line being pulled off the reel when you strike.

FEEDING THE SWIM

There is no one rule that dictates how much and how often you should introduce free offerings of bait into the swim. This will depend on a number of factors such as how many fish are in the swim and how much bait they are eating.

You will develop and instinct for feeding as you become more proficient, but at first and especially on waters you have not fished before, it is well to remember that you can always put more feed in the swim if you need to, but if you over feed you cannot take it out again.

As a general principle, it is usually better to feed 'little and often'. This well worn phrase can be translated to feeding a small number of free offerings, between five and ten is a good start, every two or three minutes.

Once you start to get bites, if they are more frequent than one every two or three minutes, you can feed every cast. Often, in well stocked stillwaters where bites are frequent, the amount you feed becomes self-regulating as the frequency of the bites determines how often you feed.

If bites slow or stop, you may need to reduce the amount you are feeding to create competition for food among the fish in your swim until bites start to come again, but do not stop feeding altogether as if all of the bait in the swim is eaten, the fish may move out of your swim in search of more.

FLOAT RIGS FOR STILLWATERS

This chapter contains diagrams of rigs and shotting patterns for stillwater float rigs covering a variety of fishing situations.

SETTING UP A STILLWATER FLOAT RIG

When fishing a stillwater fishery you will usually attach the float to the line at the bottom only, either by passing the line through a ring at the base of the float, or through a float adapter.

Most of the shot is usually used to lock the float in place by spacing it evenly on either side of the float. The remaining shot required to set or cock the float is then attached to the line below the float.

To complete the rig, a hooklength is attached using either two loops or a blood knot, both of which are explained in the chapter on fishing knots later in this book.

INSERT WAGGLER FLOAT RIG

The insert waggler is a sensitive float that can catch fish at all depths.

The bulk of the shot required to set the float should be used to lock it on to the line.

Smaller shots, number 6 or number 8, are spaced evenly down the line, finishing with a number 8 or number 10 dropper shot 5 to 10 inches from the hook.

You should strike at any indication that the float is not settling in the water.

If bites occur soon after you have cast the float, these will often not result in the float being pulled under, but instead it may move across the surface or appear to have stopped settling.

If you find that you are getting bites only after the float has settled, you can increase the rate at which the hook bait falls by moving the shot nearer the hook.

Similarly, shot can be moved nearer to the float if the fish are feeding higher in the water.

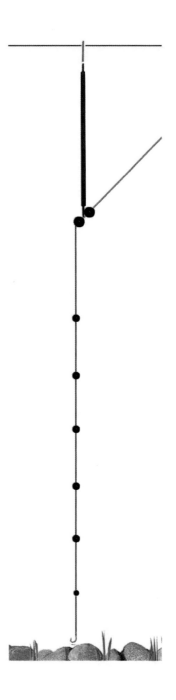

BODIED INSERT WAGGLER FLOAT RIG

The bodied insert waggler is a good choice when fish are feeding further than you can comfortably cast with a standard insert waggler.

The bulk of the shot required to set the float should be used to lock it on to the line.

Smaller shots, number 6 or number 8, are spaced evenly starting about a third of the way from the float to the hook, finishing with a number 8 or number 10 dropper shot 5 to 10 inches from the hook.

If you find that you are getting bites only after the bait has fallen almost to the bottom of the water, you can increase the rate at which the hook bait falls by moving the shot nearer the hook.

Similarly, shot can be moved nearer to the float if the fish are feeding higher in the water.

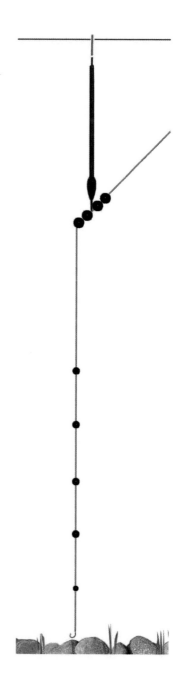

BODIED WAGGLER FLOAT RIG

The bodied waggler is an ideal float to use for distance fishing when there is a tow or strong ripple on the water.

The thicker tip helps to prevent the float from dragging under when fishing over depth and is more visible than the thinner tip of the bodied insert waggler.

The bulk of the shot required to set the float should be used to lock it on to the line.

Smaller shots, number 6 or number 8, are bulked below half depth finishing with a number 8 or number 10 dropper shot 5 to 10 inches (12 to 25 cm) from the hook.

If you find that you are getting bites 'on the drop' the shot can be moved further up the line or spaced out to provide a slower sinking hookbait.

There are occasions when fish are feeding on the bottom and will only take a static bait. If tow is causing the float to drift, this can be overcome by fishing over depth with one or two shots lying on the bottom.

WINDBEATER FLOAT RIG

If there is a very strong tow on the water, a normal waggler rig would be continually dragged under or out of position. In these conditions the windbeater enables you to fish a static bait with more sensitivity that a leger rig.

The shotting pattern is very simple; attach a single number 1 shot about 9 inches (23 cm) from the hook and lock the float to the line using the remaining shot required so that only the body is submerged and the whole stem sits out of the water.

Next plumb the depth and set the float so that 12 inches (30 cm) of line will be lying on the lake bed.

After casting, wait until the bottom shot has reached the bottom, then place the rod in two rests with the tip just under the surface and wind in until only the sight tip of the float is visible above the water.

When a fish moves the bottom shot by taking the bait, the float will rise out of the water which is your signal to strike.

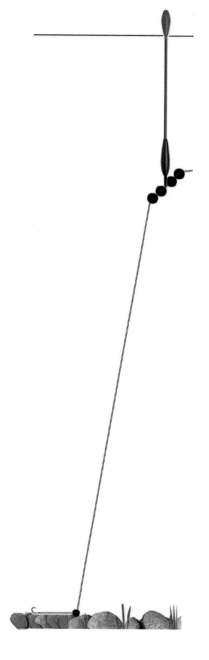

SLIDER FLOAT RIG

The slider float rig is used when the water is too deep for a fixed float rig.

A float with a large shot capacity such as a bodied waggler is required for this method.

No shot is used around the base of the float, instead the float is free running with a stop knot tied above the float at the depth of the water.

If you use a float adapter with this method it will need to be the type with a swivel to ensure the float runs freely on the line.

Shotting comprises two number 8 droppers above the hook followed by a large bulk of shot about 3 feet (90 cm) above the hook.

A further number 8 shot is placed on the line above the bulk shot for the float to rest on during casting.

After casting, wait for the bulk shot to pull through the float eye and settle before closing the bale arm and putting the rod on rests.

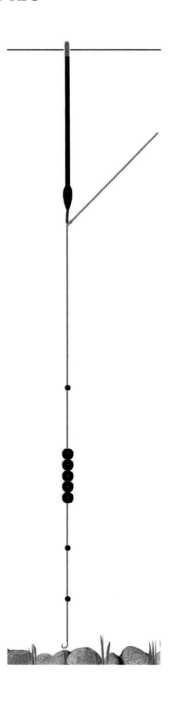

LIFT METHOD FLOAT RIG

The lift method is effective when fishing for bottom feeding fish such as tench and bream.

As the fish may not move far after picking up the hookbait, a bite may not be seen easily using a standard waggler rig.

To combat this, the float is locked on to the line using two small shots and a single shot, large enough to set the float, is placed 2 to 6 inches (5 to 15 cm) from the hook.

The depth is then accurately plumbed so that when the large shot is sitting on the bottom of the water, only the very top of the float is visible.

When a fish takes the bait, the shot will be lifted off the bottom and the float will come up in the water signalling the bite.

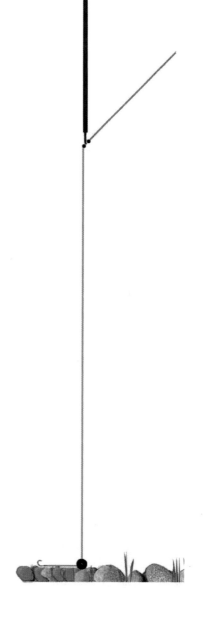

PELLET WAGGLER FLOAT RIG

The pellet waggler was developed for fishing near the surface on commercial carp fisheries.

They are normally used with hair rigs to fish with banded or drilled pellets as the bait.

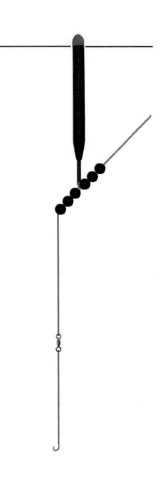

The hook length is attached to the main line using a small swivel to avoid line twist.

All of the shot required to set the float is used to lock it on the line by placing equal numbers of shot either side of the float.

As large shots are required, some anglers place thin silicon tubing either side of the float and attach the shot to the tubing to avoid the shot damaging the line.

A depth of around 2 feet (60 cm) is a good starting point, but be prepared to adjust this until you find the depth at which the fish are feeding.

Flicking the rod tip to move the float every 30 seconds or so will lift the bait and cause a disturbance which may induce a bite.

LOADED PELLET WAGGLER FLOAT RIG

The loaded pellet waggler is a variation on the standard pellet waggler that does not require any shot on the line.

Instead, a specialised pellet float adapter is used to lock the float in place.

In all other respects, the rig is the same as the standard pellet waggler rig.

The hook length is attached to the main line using a small swivel to avoid line twist.

A depth of around 2 feet (60 cm) is a good starting point, but be prepared to adjust this until you find the depth at which the fish are feeding.

Flicking the rod tip to move the float every 30 seconds or so will lift the bait and cause a disturbance which may induce a bite.

SPLASHER WAGGLER FLOAT RIG

The splasher waggler is a variation on the loaded pellet waggler that has a profile designed to maximise the disturbance or splash on the water when the float is cast into the swim.

This can be particularly effective on well stocked commercial carp fisheries where the fish have learned to associate a disturbance on the surface with food.

As with the loaded pellet waggler, a specialised pellet float adapter is used to lock the float in place and in all other respects, the rig is the same as the standard pellet waggler rig.

The hook length is attached to the main line using a small swivel to avoid line twist.

A depth of around 2 feet (60 cm) is a good starting point, but be prepared to adjust this until you find the depth at which the fish are feeding.

BAGGING WAGGLER FLOAT RIG

The bagging waggler is a version of the loaded pellet waggler that incorporates a groundbait cage at the base.

Rig construction is the same as for a loaded pellet waggler; a specialised pellet float adapter is used to lock the float in place and the hook length is attached to the main line using a small swivel to avoid line twist.

A depth of around 2 feet (60 cm) is a good starting point, but be prepared to adjust this until you find the depth at which the fish are feeding.

Each cast, a ball of method mix groundbait incorporating some samples of hook bait, is moulded on to the cage at the base of the float.

A fluffy groundbait mix is required with a consistency that does not stick to the float after it lands in the water, but is stiff enough not to come off during the cast.

MUSHROOM WAGGLER FLOAT RIG

The mushroom waggler is a version of the loaded pellet waggler designed for fishing at long distance.

A flat top is incorporated into the float to counter the tendency of a heavy float to dive under the surface when a powerful cast is required to reach the required distance.

Rig construction is the same as for a loaded pellet waggler; a specialised pellet float adapter is used to lock the float in place and the hook length is attached to the main line using a small swivel to avoid line twist.

A depth of around 2 feet (60 cm) is a good starting point, but be prepared to adjust this until you find the depth at which the fish are feeding.

CARP CONTROLLER FLOAT RIG

The carp controller float rig is suitable for fishing a floating bait when fish are feeding on the surface.

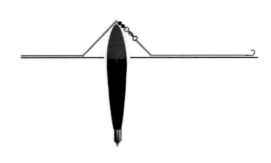

The rig is simple to construct; the main line is threaded through the eye at the top of the float, followed by one or two rubber beads that act as a shock absorber.

A size 8 swivel is then tied to the end of the main line and the hooklength is tied to the other side of the swivel.

Hair rigged floating baits such as floating pellets and bread work well with this method. Small amounts of feed should be introduced regularly. If you feed too much, wind may carry the excess bait out of your swim, followed by the fish.

Bites are detected either by watching the float for movement or watching the end of the rod tip. Bites are usually aggressive and result in the fish being hooked without the need to strike.

FLOAT FISHING ON RIVERS

When float fishing on rivers you will usually attach the float to the line using silicon or plastic tubing placed at both ends of the float. This is known as 'top and bottom' or 'double rubber'.

Shot is then attached to the line between the float and the hook, either spaced out or in bunches so that only the tip of the float is visible above the water.

The tackle is then swung out into the stream and allowed to float down the river with the current.

You need to continually pay out line with this method, so the bale arm of the reel is left open and the line is controlled by pressure applied with your finger at the edge of the spool.

To keep a tight line to the float you may need to 'mend the line' by trapping the line with your finger and lifting the rod until the line between the rod tip and float is straight. On rivers where the flow is slow and there are many surface currents you may need to do this several times on each passage of the float down the swim.

This technique is referred to as 'trotting', and when the float needs to travel a long way down the swim to reach the fish, it is known as 'long trotting'.

Although fishing at the speed of the current will usually work well, it can sometimes pay to slow the float down slightly by releasing line under gentle tension so that it moves at slightly less than the speed of the current.

Bites can sometimes be induced by holding back the float momentarily so that the hook bait lifts off the bottom.

Holding back can be particularly effective if done at the end of the swim before reeling in to make the next cast.

When you get a bite, trap the line against the spool with your finger and strike with a sweeping movement away from the float. The further away the float is, the more powerful the strike, but often it is only necessary to stop the float as the current will set the hook.

Another river float fishing method involves the use of a waggler float that is only attached to the line at the bottom. This allows the float to be cast further without risk of tangles on wide rivers, or when you want to fish near the far bank.

With this method it is not possible to keep a tight line to the float as this would cause it to be pulled towards you and the bait would not appear to be behaving naturally to the fish.

Instead of mending the line, you allow a bow to form between the rod tip and float, and you then 'feed the bow' by paying out enough line to allow the float to move unhindered down the swim.

A more powerful strike is required with this method as you have to recover all of the line in the bow before making contact with the fish. This is achieved by a high sweeping movement of the rod over your shoulder.

With both methods, as soon as a fish is hooked you have to decide whether you need to allow it to take line before you close the bail arm of the reel in preparation for winding in or playing the fish. If it is a small fish you can immediately close the bail arm and commence winding. If you feel resistance from a large fish, allow it to take line with the bail arm open, and close it only when you feel the fish stop its initial run.

When fishing with running line tackle on rivers, make sure that the anti-reverse on the reel is set to the off position if you intend to give line by winding backwards rather than using the slipping clutch.

CHOOSING WHICH FLOAT TO USE

As a general rule your choice of float will be dictated by the speed of the current, the depth of the river and other factors such as wind.

So long as you do not need to cast a considerable distance, for example to the far bank on a wide river, and there is not a strong downstream wind, you will usually choose one of the patterns of float that is attached to the line at both the top and the bottom.

Long casting is not really practical with a 'top and bottom' attached float and such floats are difficult to control in a downstream wind, so in either case you would usually be best fishing with a straight waggler attached 'bottom only'. If the wind is so strong that even a straight waggler is difficult to fish, this may be one of those occasions when legering is the only practical method.

So long as you are fishing a comfortable casting distance from your own bank and there is no wind or it is blowing upstream, one of the patterns of 'top and bottom' float described earlier should be suitable.

If you are fishing with a very large bait, such as a slug or lobworm, the extra stability provided by a chubber float would make it the right choice, but this is quite a specialist method employed by anglers who are selective about the size and species of fish they want to catch. Most of the time, a stick float, balsa or avon will be suitable.

Float selection is covered in more detail in the following chapter describing river float rigs but as a general guide, for deep and slow flowing rivers where you need to use a large amount of shot to get the bait to the bottom quickly you would usually choose an Avon style float. At the opposite extreme where a river is flowing very fast, a balsa would be the right choice and in all other conditions, a stick float should perform well.

FINDING THE DEPTH OF YOUR SWIM

If you are fishing a slow moving river, the depth of the swim can be found using a plummet as described in the chapter on stillwater fishing.

On faster moving water a plummet cannot be used as the float will be pulled under by the flow so it is necessary instead to set the float at your best guess of the depth and run the float through the swim several times, adjusting the depth each time until the hook catches on the river bed and the float is pulled under.

Finally slide the float back towards the float a little and run the float though the swim again to make sure that it will reach the end of the swim without the hook catching on the bottom.

Some swims can vary in depth throughout their length. Here you have two choices:

- Set the float to a depth that will allow the hook to clear the bottom throughout the length of the swim.

- Set the float to a depth where it will only catch the bottom occasionally, and as the float reaches those areas hold it back slightly to cause the hook to rise above the bottom until the float has passed into deeper water.

FEEDING THE SWIM

Feeding a swim on a river is quite different to feeding a swim on a stillwater.

Depending on the depth of the swim and the strength of the current, your bait could reach the river bed anywhere from just past the point at which you introduce it, to a significant distance down the river.

Over time you will develop a feel for where in the swim, or even above it, you will need to introduce free offerings, but as a general guide, the faster the flow and the deeper the swim, the further upstream you will need to introduce bait.

You should aim for your bait to reach the bottom of the river about two thirds of the way down the swim. The bait will continue to move with the current after it reaches the bottom, but by this time your hookbait should also be travelling near the bottom.

As a general rule you should feed every cast and just before you cast so that your hookbait is travelling among the free offerings. The 'little and often' principle described in the chapter on stillwater fishing applies and is even more important when fishing rivers as you want to attract fish into the swim and keep them there, not chasing off downstream after excess bait.

It may take some time for you to start getting bites if there are few fish in the swim to begin with, but eventually fish should be drawn upstream by your loose feed and once they are in the swim, feeding small amounts of bait regularly should keep them there.

FLOAT RIGS FOR RIVERS

This chapter contains diagrams of rigs and shotting patterns for river float rigs covering a variety of fishing situations.

SETTING UP A RIVER FLOAT RIG

When fishing a river you will usually attach the float to the line at both the top and bottom using silicon tubing. The exception to this is when you are fishing with a waggler float, in which case the float is attached 'bottom only' as described in the previous chapter.

When fishing with bodied floats or floats with a thin wire stem and additional length of tubing is also attached to the float just below the body.

The shot required to set or cock the float is then attached to the line below the float.

To complete the rig, a hooklength is attached using either two loops or a blood knot, both of which are explained in the chapter on fishing knots later in this book.

STICK FLOAT RIG

The basic stick float rig is suitable for medium paced rivers up to 7 feet deep.

The float is attached to the line using two pieces of silicon tubing. For wire stemmed stick floats a third piece of tubing is used at the base of the balsa body.

The shot required to set the float is made up of several shots, size 4, 6 or 8 depending on the capacity of the float, spaced evenly down the line.

The float should be allowed to travel through the swim at the speed of the current. Mend the line as necessary to keep a straight line to the float so it is not dragged or pulled out of position by the current.

Bites can sometimes be induced by holding back the float momentarily from time to time so the bait lifts in the water.

Shotting can be adjusted by bunching the shots together if a slower or faster falling bait is required by conditions on the day.

DEEP WATER STICK FLOAT RIG

The deep water stick float rig is suitable for medium paced rivers over 7 feet deep.

The float is attached to the line using two pieces of silicon tubing. For wire stemmed stick floats a third piece of tubing is used at the base of the balsa body.

The shot required to set the float is made up of bunches of size 4, 6 or 8 shots depending on the capacity of the float, spaced evenly down the lower half of the line.

The float should be allowed to travel through the swim at the speed of the current. Mend the line as necessary to keep a straight line to the float so it is not dragged or pulled out of position by the current.

Bites can sometimes be induced by holding back the float momentarily from time to time so the bait lifts in the water.

BALSA FLOAT RIG

The balsa float rig is suitable for fast flowing rivers.

The float is attached to the line using two pieces of silicon tubing.

The shot required to set the float is made up of bunches of shots spaced evenly down the lower half of the line. Depending on the shot capacity of the float and the speed of the current, quite large shots, up to number 1 or BB may be required.

For very fast flows where the fish are feeding very close to the bottom, it may be necessary to bunch all of the shots together a few inches above the dropper shot.

The float should be controlled through the swim usually at the speed of the current, but it can sometimes be effective to release line under tension so the float travels slightly slower.

Mend the line as necessary to keep a straight line to the float so it is not dragged or pulled out of position by the current.

AVON FLOAT RIG

The avon float rig is suitable for fishing at close range in deep rivers with a medium to fast flow.

The float is attached to the line using three pieces of silicon tubing placed at the top and bottom of the float and just below the body.

Shotting consists of a bunch of large shot, AAA or BB depending on the shotting capacity of the float about 2 feet (30 cm) from the hook, and a smaller dropper shot.

On entering the water, the bulk of large shot will quickly take the hook bait to the bottom and the float is them allowed to move through the swim at the speed of the current.

Mend the line as necessary to keep a straight line to the float so it is not dragged or pulled out of position by the current.

Bites can sometimes be induced by slowing down the float or holding it back momentarily from time to time so the bait lifts in the water.

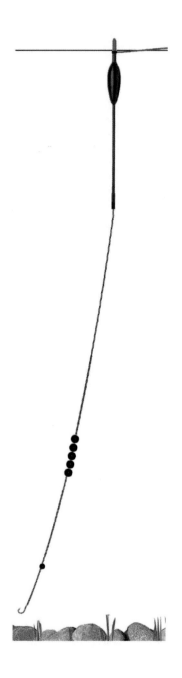

CHUBBER FLOAT RIG

The chubber float rig is suitable for fishing fast flowing shallow rivers with large baits such as worms and bread.

The float is attached to the line using two pieces of silicon tubing.

The shot required to set the float is made up of a single bunch of large shot, AAA or SSG depending on the shot carrying capacity of the float, with a single dropper, number 4 or number 6, near the hook.

The float should be controlled through the swim usually at the speed of the current, but it can sometimes be effective to release line under tension so the float travels slightly slower.

Mend the line as necessary to keep a straight line to the float so it is not dragged or pulled out of position by the current.

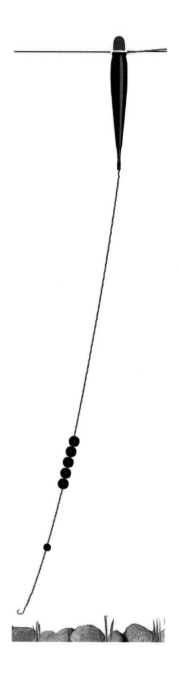

STRAIGHT WAGGLER FLOAT RIG

The straight waggler float rig is suitable for medium to fast flowing rivers where a long cast is required or a downstream wind prevents use of a stick float.

Most of the shot required to set the float is used to lock it on the line at the base. The remaining shot is made up of number 6 or number 8 shots spaced evenly down the line, one shot for every two feet of depth, plus a number 8 dropper shot.

The float needs to travel through the swim naturally at the speed of the current, but the technique of mending the line used with floats attached top and bottom would drag the float under.

Instead, allow a bow to form between the rod tip and float and feed the bow by paying out enough line to allow the float to move unhindered down the swim.

A powerful strike is required with this method as you have to recover all of the line in the bow before making contact with the fish.

SPECI-WAGGLER FLOAT RIG

The speci-waggler float rig is suitable for medium to fast flowing rivers where a long cast is required and a shorter float is required than would be needed if a standard straight was used.

Most of the shot required to set the float is used to lock it on the line at the base. The remaining shot is made up of number 4 shots spaced evenly down the line, one shot for every two feet of depth, plus a number 6 dropper shot.

The float needs to travel through the swim naturally at the speed of the current. Due to the extra thickness and buoyancy of this float, mending the line is usually possible without moving the float out of position.

If conditions make mending the line difficult on the day, allow a bow to form between the rod tip and float and feed the bow by paying out enough line to allow the float to move unhindered down the swim. .

CASTING TECHNIQUES

There are two main casting techniques that you will need to master, the overhead cast, and the underarm cast.

You would normally use the overhead cast when fishing 'bottom only' and the underhand cast when you are fishing 'top and bottom' but there are no hard and fast rules about which cast you should use for a given situation and you will quickly develop your own style.

,As a general rule, use the overhead cast when you need to cast a long distance, and the underarm cast when long distance casting is not required or you are fishing with tackle such as a stick float rig that could easily tangle if you used an overhead cast.

OVERHEAD CAST

This is probably the easier of the two to learn as timing is less important than with the underhand cast. A poorly timed overhead cast will, unless it is really badly mis-timed, just result in less distance and a bigger splash when the tackle hits the water.

To begin the cast, let out enough line so that you can comfortably swing the tackle by moving the rod backwards and forwards. Open the bail arm of the spool so that the line can run off, and prevent this by trapping the line against the spool with your finger.

Next, lift the rod to a vertical position so that it is pointing straight up. The next part requires practice to get the timing just right so don't worry if your initial attempts don't go too well.

Imagine that you are standing next to a large clock face, and the rod is currently pointing to 12 o'clock.

In one fluid movement, swing the tackle behind you by moving the rod sharply back so that it is pointing at between 10 and 11 o'clock, and then immediately move the rod sharply forwards so that it is pointing at between 1 and 2 o'clock. Stop the rod, and release the line by lifting your finger off the spool.

If you get the timing right, the tackle should be propelled away from you towards the place where you want to fish and if the spool is loaded correctly, line should come off the spool freely.

When the tackle is a few inches above the water, drop the rod tip to between 3 and 4 o'clock, and the tackle should land gently on the surface without causing too much disturbance.

The most difficult part of the cast is timing the release of the line correctly. If you release too early, the line will fly up in the air without the necessary power, and will land in a heap. Release too late, and the tackle will not achieve the required distance and will be driven with excessive force into the water.

UNDERHAND CAST

This cast will not achieve the same distance as the overhead cast, but it does give you more control over the tackle in flight and is less likely to result in the tackle becoming tangled.

To begin the cast, assuming you are right handed, hold the rod in your right hand, open the bail arm of the reel, and let out enough line from the rod tip so that with your left hand you can comfortably hold the line just above the hook.

Hold the rod across your body while keeping the line under tension with your left hand, and then flick the rod towards the water so that it is pointing directly away from you, at the same time releasing the line held in your left hand. You should find that the tackle is propelled towards the place you want to fish, and if you get enough power into the cast, and get your timing right, line should flow off the spool.

Timing of this cast is quite difficult to master, but with practice you will find that it becomes second nature. As your skills progress you will find that you can achieve this cast holding the rod at different angles to avoid bank side vegetation and other obstacles.

PLAYING, LANDING AND RELEASING FISH

Much of the information in this chapter is not specifically about float fishing and can be applied to any fishing method.

STRIKING OR SETTING THE HOOK

Striking is the term used to describe the action of setting the hook in the fish when you get a bite.

It is not usually necessary to do more than move the rod swiftly back a few inches with a flick, but when fishing at range, or if there is a lot of slack line between you and your tackle, you may need to strike with a sweeping action to pick up the slack line and make contact with the fish.

Speed of the strike is much more important than power as all you are trying to do is pull the hook firmly into the mouth of the fish before it has time to eject the bait.

As a general rule, keep in mind that the closer in you are fishing, the less powerfully you need to strike.

An unnecessarily powerful strike when fishing at close range will result in your tackle being pulled out of the water, sometimes with a small fish attached! There is no surer way that I know of to get your tackle in a tangle!

PLAYING FISH

Small fish can be wound in quite easily and then swung to hand, but large fish are capable of long sustained fights during which you may have to give line.

When you hook a large fish, do not try to bully it out of the water as quickly as possible, your aim is to tire the fish so that when all of the fight has gone out of it, you can draw it safely over the landing net.

Large fish will try to swim away from you as fast as they can when they are hooked, or soon after as they feel resistance. You will usually need to give line to prevent a break or the hook pulling free and this can be done in two ways.

Most reels are equipped with a slipping clutch. This allows the spool to rotate to give line when the pull is approaching that which would break the line. An alternative is to allow the fish to take line under pressure by winding the reel backwards. Many anglers use a combination of the two, using judgment to determine when giving line by back winding is necessary.

If you do choose to use the slipping clutch, make sure it is set to just below the breaking strain of the line. Too slack and you will struggle to recover line, too tight and you risk a break.

Playing a fish is a little like a tug of war match. You give a little, you gain a little until eventually the fish is tired. To gain the maximum advantage from your tackle it is essential that you use the rod to cushion the lunges of the fish, so most of the time you should hold it high. This applies maximum pressure on the fish, and also prevents it from coming too high in the water before it is ready for the net.

The exception to this is when you need to stop a fish from reaching an obstruction such as a weed bed or some tree roots. If you lock down the reel and try to stop the fish by holding the rod high you may pull out the hook or break the line. When you need to stop a fish in this way, drop the rod tip so you are applying 'side strain'. Usually this will force the fish up nearer the surface and is often enough to make it change direction away from the snag.

Learning to play a fish well is something that only experience can teach you, but with perseverance you will develop an instinct for when a fish is ready to be brought to the net.

LANDING FISH

When a fish is tired you will notice that its lunges and runs become weaker and shorter. This can be the most dangerous part of the fight, as the fish will be closer and nearer the surface and you have only a short amount of line between you and the fish.

Very often, a fish that has been brought to the surface will make a desperate lunge for freedom as soon as it sees you or the net, so be prepared to give more line and continue the fight when this happens.

Eventually the fish will be beaten and will turn sideways on the surface. Now is the time to slip the net under the fish and draw it back from the water.

Do not drag the fish for a long distance to the net, try to get the net as close to the fish and draw it over the lip of the net in a steady controlled movement. When fishing fast rivers you may need to position the net a little downstream of the fish, and allow the current to take the fish over the net. Never try to pull a beaten fish against the current as that is a sure way of pulling out the hook.

Once the fish is in the net, draw the net back in the water to ensure the fish is safely in the folds. You should then disengage the bale arm on the reel and place the rod in its rest so you have both hands free to lift the net.

Do not lift the net out of the water while you are still holding the end of the pole as it will bend, and could break. Instead, slide the pole backwards until you can safely lift it out of the water by gripping the pole with both hands near the net.

UNHOOKING FISH

Small fish can be safely unhooked in the hand after being swung in, larger fish should be unhooked while lying on the bank supported on a soft surface such as an unhooking mat.

Be careful when unhooking fish not to grip them too tightly, and only handle them with damp hands to prevent removal of slime.

Most of the time a fish will be hooked in the lip, and the hook can be easily removed by hand. Grip the shank of the hook between finger and thumb and gently pull it out. Barbless hooks will come out easily, but barbed hooks may need to be removed by very gently shaking the hook at the same time as pulling to release the grip of the barb.

If the fish is hooked deeper in the mouth and you cannot reach it with your fingers, you may need to use forceps to grimly grip the hook to remove it using the same technique as above.

USING A DISGORGER

When a fish has swallowed the hook and you cannot see it to grip it with forceps you will need to use a disgorger. You should make sure that you have several of these in your fishing kit and jacket so you can quickly lay your hands on one when needed. Some anglers have a disgorger on a piece of string round their neck, or on a cord attached to their jacket so it is close to hand.

A disgorger is simple to use, but takes a little practice. Keep the line under gentle tension by wrapping it around a finger of the hand that is holding the disgorger. Then, slide the disgorger on to the line using the slot in the side, and gently push the disgorger down the line until you feel the resistance of the hook.

A further gentle push should dislodge the hook, and you should then turn the disgorger a little and pull it back out of the fish. It should come out with no resistance, so if it will not come out easily, the hook has not been dislodged and you need to repeat the process.

RETURNING FISH TO THE WATER

It is important that you do not throw fish back into the water as they are fragile creatures and could be damaged. Instead, gently slip the fish into the water head first and it should swim away strongly.

On high banks you may not be able to reach the water, so return the fish by lowering it to the surface in your landing net and gently turning it out.

Some fish, notably Barbel, need time to recover before they can swim away and you may need to support them with their heads pointed into the current until you feel them swim away from you.

If you use a keep net, release the fish at the end of the session by gently lifting the end of the net furthest from the mouth so the fish swim out. Do not allow fish to flap around in the bottom of a net out of water as the larger fish will damage themselves, and other smaller fish below them.

If you want to weigh your fish after a session you will need to remove them from the net while it is out of water. Some keep nets have a ring that allows the bottom of the net to be lifted out of the mouth so fish can be removed safely.

If your keep net does not have this feature, move the fish as near to the mouth of the net as possible using the method in the previous paragraph before gently tipping them into the weighing net. The head of a landing net can be used to weigh fish if you do not have a specialist weighing net or basket.

KNOTS FOR FISHING

There are many knots that are suitable for fishing, but you need only learn a few to begin with to be equipped for any float fishing situation.

When tying knots it is a good idea to moisten the knot before pulling tight as this will lubricate the line and prevent it from being weakened by heat damage caused by friction.

JOINING TWO LENGTHS OF LINE

There are two common methods for joining two lengths of line, e.g. to attach a short length of lighter hook length line to the main line.

LOOP METHOD

The simplest method of joining two lengths of line is to use two loops tied using a surgeon's loop knot.

SURGEON'S LOOP KNOT

To tie a surgeons loop knot, first double the line back on itself to form a loop. Next form a loop using the doubled line and pass the end through this larger loop two or three times. Finally, moisten the line and pull tight.

STEP 1   STEP 2   STEP 3

JOINING THE TWO LOOPS

Thread the loops together as shown and pull tight.

BLOOD KNOT

An alternative method that you can use when you do not want to use loops is the blood knot.

ATTACHING HOOKS TO LINE

Hooks that are not purchased already tied to line can be attached using the knots illustrated below. Small spade end hooks are more easily tied using a hook tyer, an inexpensive accessory available from fishing tackle shops.

SNELL KNOT

This knot can be used to tie either eyed or spade end hooks. If tying an eyed hook, first pass the line through the eye of the hook.

TUCKED HALF BLOOD KNOT

The tucked half blood knot can be used to attach eyed hooks and swivels to line.

STEP 1   STEP 2   STEP 3

STOP KNOT

The stop knot is used when typing a slider rig described in the chapter on stillwater float rigs.

STEP 1   STEP 2   STEP 3

LICENCES AND PERMISSION TO FISH

Anyone aged 12 or over must have a fishing licence to fish for coarse fish. The penalty for being caught fishing without a licence is a fine of up to £2,500.

Full details of current prices can be obtained from the Environment Agency website, where you can also apply for a licence. Licences can also be obtained at post offices.

A licence only allows you to fish legally, it does not mean you can fish anywhere you choose. There are some locations where you can fish for free, but most fishing waters are either owned by fishing clubs that you have to join, or available to fish by purchasing a day ticket.

WHEN YOU CAN FISH

On rivers there is an annual close season for coarse fishing from 15 March to 15 June each year and you are not allowed to fish using coarse fishing methods during that period.

There is no close season for coarse fishing on lakes, canals and ponds so you are legally allowed to fish all year round, but some clubs enforce their own close season, so check the rules for your chosen fishery before setting out.

If you intend to fish at night, which can be a very productive time for many species, check with your local club or fishery to find out if this is allowed, and whether you need to obtain a special night fishing permit.

ACKNOWLEDGMENTS

Image of Fishing Reel: Original photo by Jan Tik: http://www.flickr.com/people/jantik/. Vectorized version by Chabacano: http://commons.wikimedia.org/wiki/User: Chabacano, licensed under the Creative Commons Attribution ShareAlike 2.5, Attribution ShareAlike 2.0 and Attribution ShareAlike 1.0 License.

ABOUT THE AUTHOR

As someone who was born in the middle part of the last century, before video games, colour television and the many other electronic distractions of today I have fond memories of the time that I spent reading old fishing books, making fishing tackle, and learning to catch fish in the local stream.

There were few 'commercial fisheries' then. Waters were, by and large, in a natural state and not stocked to the brim with artificially reared carp of uniform size that will compete for any food thrown at them. In fact, Carp were considered the most difficult fish to catch, whereas today if you want to catch a fish of more than a few ounces, its probably easier to catch a carp than anything else.

I get as much pleasure, maybe more, from catching a few small fish from a tiny unspoilt river, as from 'bagging up' on a well stocked artificial pond. Coarse fishing, if practiced in a more traditional way, has infinite variety, and success is not measured by the number or size of fish caught alone.

Paul Duffield

Printed in Great Britain
by Amazon